Please Don't Forget About Me Tea For My Soul

Jaydin C Donough

Published by Jaydin Donough, 2024.

2. Copyright Page

© 2024 Jaydin C Donough Silent Writer

All rights reserved. No part of this book may be reproduced, distributed, or transmitted in any form or by any means, without the prior written permission of the author.

Please Don't Forget About Me Tea For My Soul!!

Authors: Silent writer, Jaydin C Donough

Publisher: Jaydin Donough

Tales of Nature Lost Among the Thorns

ISBN: 978-1-0370-2091-9(print)

While every precaution has been taken in the preparation of this book, the publisher assumes no responsibility for errors or omissions, or for damages resulting from the use of the information contained herein.

PLEASE DON'T FORGET ABOUT ME TEA FOR MY SOUL

First edition. November 6, 2024.

Copyright © 2024 Jaydin C Donough.

ISBN: 978-1037020933

Written by Jaydin C Donough.

Also by Jaydin C Donough

Please Don't Forget About Me Tea For My Soul
Tales of Nature Lost among the Thorns

In a world full of noise, I write for you, the one who hears the quiet within."

— Jaydin C Donough, Silent Writer

Acknowledgments

To my family, for your unwavering support, and to my friends, for inspiring me to push through when the words didn't come easily. To those who believed in this book, I'm forever grateful for your encouragement and faith.

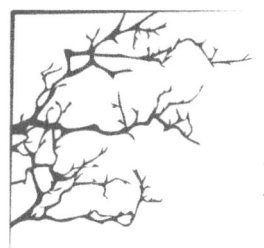

Dedication

To the one I have yet to meet, the one whose presence I've already felt long before our paths cross. I thought of you in every word, in every moment of these poems. You are the personification of love—an idea I held onto, a feeling I sought. When we finally meet, I hope you understand that I have been waiting for you all along.

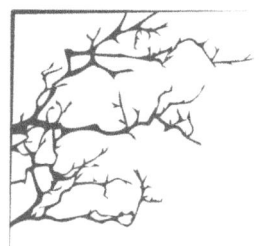

Foreword

Love is a journey we all take, though not always at the same time. For me, this journey has been about more than just the love I've experienced; it's been about the love I've yet to find. In writing these poems, I imagined you—someone whose presence has yet to fill the spaces of my life, but whose essence I have always known.
This collection is a tribute to the feeling of waiting for that one person who will be the embodiment of everything I've dreamt of—an eternal love, a connection that transcends time. Though we haven't met yet, I have written these words for you, as a testament to the kind of love I believe in. A love that exists even before we know the face or the voice of the one who will carry it.
I hope these words resonate with anyone who has felt that longing, that hope for something more. For you, the one who will one day read this and recognize yourself in these pages—know that I've been waiting for you. And when we meet, I hope you see the love that has always been here for you, waiting patiently in the lines of these poems.
Jaydin C Donough Silent Writer

Chapter 1: The Spaces Between Us

"In the spaces where words fail, love speaks the loudest. It's in the quiet moments, the in-betweens, where we truly find one another."

The Spaces Between Us

In the silence between heartbeats,
I find you—
Not in the loudness of life,
But in the quiet moments,
Where the world fades,
And it's just us.
You are the breath I take
When the weight of the world presses down,
The calm in the storm that rages inside me.
I wonder—how can something so fragile,
So delicate,
Be the only thing that makes me feel whole?
There are days I fear you'll slip away,
Like sand through my fingers,
Leaving nothing but the memory
Of your touch,
Your laugh,
The way your eyes hold the sky.
I've never known love like this before—
It terrifies me,
And yet, I crave it.
To love you is to walk a tightrope,
To dance on the edge of everything,
Knowing that at any moment, I could fall,
And still, I'd risk it all for you.
Because you are the spaces between every word I say,
The reason I wake before the sun,
Just to watch you dream,
To remind myself that this is real.

You are the reflection of everything I've ever wanted,
Everything I never knew I needed.
And though I may not always say it,
May not always show it,
I love you beyond words,
Beyond time,

Beyond this lifetime.
If I could carve my heart into the stars,
I would—
So even when I am nothing but dust,
You'll look up,
And know
That I loved you
With every piece of me
That ever was.

If You Only Knew
If you only knew
How every quiet thought is filled with you—
In moments when the world is too loud,
And I retreat into the silence of my mind,
It's your face I see,
Your voice that brings calm
To the chaos inside me.
If you only knew
The weight of your name
On my tongue,
The way it lingers like a prayer
I've said a thousand times,
Hoping the universe listens,
Hoping you feel it too.
If you only knew
How your laughter is the soundtrack
To the life I wish to lead—
Carefree, yet purposeful,
A reminder that even in the darkest hours,
There's light if I have you.
If you only knew
The way I see the future—
Painted in the soft hues of your smile,
Framed by the certainty of your love.
I see us, standing at the edge of forever,
And I know,
This is where I am meant to be.
If you only knew
How the smallest things—

Your glance,
Your touch,
Your presence—
Are enough to fill every empty space
Inside of me.
You've woven yourself into the fabric of my soul,
And I am better for it.
If you only knew...
How much you mean to me,
How every breath I take,
Every choice I make,
Is made with you in mind.
Maybe then,
You'd understand why I am
The way I am
When it comes to you.

Beneath the Quiet Moon

In the stillness of night,
I listen for your breath—
But all I hear is silence.
The moon hangs heavy, watching over us,
Its pale light a reminder
Of how far we've drifted.
Once, you were the warmth beside me,
But now you're the dream
I can never reach,
A shadow on the edge of my mind,
Fading with every passing moment.
I count the stars,
Each one a promise we made—

Now scattered, broken.
How do I hold on to what slips through my fingers
Like water, like time?
I search for you in the spaces
Between the seconds,
In the breath before dawn,
But all I find is the empty echo
Of your name.

To Love Thee is to Wait

To love thee is to wait with quiet breath,
While days and nights doth pass me slowly by.
In every waking hour, fear of death,
For shouldst thou leave, what soul would I be nigh?
I see thee in the shadows of the day,
Thy voice a distant echo in the air.
Wouldst thou remain, my heart shall never stray,
But absent thou, my love turns to despair.
So take my hand, and never let me go,
For time is cruel, and love is but a game.
Yet in thy arms, the world will never know,
Of all the fear that dare not speak thy name.
For in thy touch, I find both loss and gain,
A love that giveth all, yet taketh pain.

HOLD

Hold me close when the night turns cold,
Open your heart to let me in.
Love me like the stories told—
Don't let the silence win.

Between Heartbeats
It's in the pauses that I feel you most,
Between the heartbeats,
In the moments where time stops
And we are nothing
But the space between breaths.

The Unspoken Word

In every word left unsaid,
There is a world of feeling
That I cannot find the courage to speak.
I tell you that I love you
Not with words,
But with the way I trace your name
Into the air
When you're not looking,
The way my hand reaches for you
In my dreams,
As though you are the air I need to breathe.
I wonder,
If silence holds more power than words,
If in the spaces between us,
You hear what I've never said.

The Fragility of Us

Your love is like glass in my hands,
Beautiful, but fragile,
shattering as it lands.

Message in the Bottle

Each word I send is a small anchor,
Cast into the ocean of time,
Driven by currents unseen,
Drifting until it finds you,
Somewhere, someday.
In every letter, I leave whispers,
Soft traces of my heart's quiet song,
A love adrift on waves and tides,
Waiting for shores I have never known.
If you hold it close, perhaps you'll feel
A memory that isn't yours,
Some echo of hands once intertwined,
Of laughter shared in hidden places,
Of lives that our hearts may remember,
Even if we don't yet know how to say it.
These words are my lanterns on darkened seas,
Cast out, searching for you, across the years,
Waiting, patiently, for the moment
When you might catch their faint glow.

Unwritten Letter

I hold back the words I want to say,
For they're better saved for you,
In a time yet untouched by this day.
Ink trembles on paper, carrying secrets,
Stories I have kept hidden,
Tender verses, safe in the quiet of waiting.
Each letter lies between empty pages—
Hushed, as though they're holding their breath,
Longing to find their voice through you.

As if in each line, I leave a piece of me,
Pieces that may one day find you
Across the distance, in a world
Where love finally learns your name.
When the time is right, perhaps they'll come alive,
In the warmth of your hands.

The Invisible Thread

An unseen line between us grows,
Though I know not where it begins
Or where it ends—
Only that I feel its pull,
Steady, certain, silent.
This thread winds softly, like a river through stone,
A tether spun by fate, binding us
In places neither of us has ever known.
Like stardust that drifts unseen,
This delicate line stretches across eons,
Linking every breath, every heartbeat,
To a space between souls, unseen.
As though we have always belonged
To a bond beyond ourselves—
Something greater, something whole,
Something that, no matter how far we go,
Will always pull us home.

Whispers Across the Miles

Each thought of you drifts like a whisper,
Carried across unseen miles,
Landing softly in the space
Only you will ever know.
My heart speaks, though silent to all,
These quiet messages, cast adrift,
Waiting to reach you in the stillness.
In every passing cloud,
In each whisper of wind,
My soul reaches for yours,
In hopes that you'll feel me there.

Silent Companion

I walk through shadows alone,
Yet feel your presence beside me,
A quiet companion in my solitude,
A steady warmth in the dark.
In each unspoken word,
In every unshed tear,
You are the echo of every step,
The heartbeat that follows mine,
As if you've been here all along,
Lighting my path with an unseen flame.
So even in the quietest moments,
I am never truly alone,
For you are my constant,
My silent companion.

Unfamiliar Familiar

I feel as though I've known you before,
Though we've never met—
A stranger, and yet,
The most familiar part of me.
Perhaps in another lifetime,
We crossed paths a thousand times,
Exchanging glances in worlds long past,
And each time, I knew you,
As if you were always meant to be mine.
You are the piece that has waited within me,
For a reunion, timeless and true,
And though our paths have yet to cross,
I recognize you in the spaces of my heart,
As though you have always been there.

Chapter 2: Timeless Love

"Love is not bound by time; it's the thread that weaves through every moment, creating something eternal in its wake."

Death Struck Me Not
Death struck me not,
Death, where is thy victory?
Hades, where is thy sting?
For I stand before thee,
Unbowed, unbroken—
My wife, my queen,
Her love shields me from your reach.
I tellest thee,
That death struck me not,
For I have seen the light
Within her eyes,
A fire that burns brighter
Than your shadow could ever hope to cast.
You sought to claim me,
But found me untouchable,
For her love has wrapped itself
Around my soul,
An armor forged in eternity,
Stronger than any grave.
Death, tremble at her name—
For where she walks,
Life follows,
And I, her devoted,
Am beyond your grasp.
I tellest thee again,
That death struck me not,
For in her arms,
I am immortal,
Her love, my crown,

Her heart, my kingdom.

A Love Beyond the Stars

Thine eyes, like stars, shine ever in the night,
A beacon through the endless, darkened skies.
And though the world may turn from day to night,
In thee, I find the sun that never dies.
Through time, through death, through all that fades away,
Thy love remains, a flame that ne'er grows dim.
Though fleeting moments pass, and years decay,
My heart shall beat with thine in timeless hymn.
For love is not a thing that time may steal,
Nor breaketh it beneath the weight of years.
In thee, I find a love that makes me feel
Immortal, free from all of time's cruel fears.
Thus, in thy arms, I know no end, no death,
For love shall ever outlast mortal breath.

Eternal Echoes

In the quiet of eternity,
Your name is a whisper
That never fades.
It moves through the ages,
Dancing on the winds of time,
Carving itself into the stars.
Even when the world falls silent,
When the weight of centuries
Has erased every memory,
Your name will remain,
Etched into the very fabric of the universe.
Time cannot touch what we've become—
We are echoes,
Endless,
Unfading.
In every heartbeat,
I feel your pulse,
And in every breath,
I carry your soul.

Time's Cruel Hands

Time, relentless as the sea,
In waves it steals the years away.
My love for thee shall ever be,
Even when our bones decay.

The Hourglass

The grains of time
Slip through my fingers,
Each one a moment we've lost,
Yet still, I hold onto you,
For though time takes all,
Our love remains
Untouched,
Timeless.

The Weight of Forever
_Beneath endless skies,
Our love defies every clock,
Forever bound still.

A Love Without Time

Time cannot hold us.
We are not bound by its ticking hands
Nor by the rise and fall of seasons.
Our love is a force,
Unchanged by the turning of the earth,
Untouched by the weight of years.
It lingers in the space
Where past meets future,
Where the now becomes forever.
In your eyes,
I find a moment that stretches
Into infinity—
A love that neither time nor death
Can claim.

To the Ends of Time

I pledge to thee, my heart, for all of time,
And though the years may pass, our love shall stay.
The weight of age will ne'er be mine or thine,
For in each breath, we'll find another day.
When stars do fall and oceans cease to roar,
And all the world succumbs to silent night,
Still shall I love thee, just as once before,
A flame that burns despite the fading light.
So take my hand, and journey past the stars,
Where we, as one, will find no end, no start.
No force of time or fate our love shall mar,
For thou art ever etched within my heart.

Bound by Eternity
Forever
Woven in time,
We spin, we turn,
We fall into the night,
Yet we rise again,
Without end.

Fossil of Us

If these words were stones,
They'd settle in the sand,
Waiting to be unearthed,
A fossil of the love I felt for you.
In layers, buried by time,
Our moments would be pressed,
Preserved in the heart of the earth,
Waiting to be found, to breathe anew.
Each line a delicate imprint,
Embossed upon the ages,
A love preserved, unchanged,
Long after we are dust and memory.

Echo of Tomorrow
In each line, I leave an echo,
A trace of me that even time
Cannot erase, in hopes
It reaches you one day.
My love stretches through time,
Like sound sent into a canyon,
Waiting for a voice to return
The sound of us.
In every syllable lies a future,
An unspoken tomorrow,
Where we are still here,
Forever resounding.

The Star Left Behind

My love for you is a star,
Born ages ago, shining still.
By the time it finds you,
It may no longer burn—
Yet its light will always reach you.
When you look up and see it glimmer,
Know that somewhere in its glow
Is a piece of me, reaching for you.
A light that defies distance,
That stretches across eons,
So even if I fade,
Its memory shines on

Eternal Flame
Even if the stars burn out,
Our love will continue to glow,
A soft, unending flame
In the quiet of eternity.
For time may take its toll,
But it cannot touch what we've become—
A spark that refuses to die.
Through shadows and silence,
In the spaces where light fades,
We remain, bound and blazing,
An immortal warmth in the endless night.

The Keeper of Time
You hold my memories as though they were your own,
Keeping every moment safe
From the wear and tear of years.
In you, I find a keeper,
A guardian of time,
For in each breath you take,
You carry my past, present, and future.
You are the clock that never stops,
The hand that never falters,
Keeping us alive through each tick of eternity.

A Century's Kiss

If I could love you through a hundred lifetimes,
I would, without pause—
For you are worth every moment.
A love like this, unbound by time,
Knows no limit, no end,
Only the echo of a kiss that spans centuries.
Through ages of silence and waiting,
I would seek you, across realms,
For a thousand lifetimes, just to find you again.

Chapter 3: Nature and Balance

"Love is like the earth—rooted, yet always reaching for the light. It moves in cycles, a perfect balance between giving and receiving."

Yin-Yang
Cycles,
Light and dark,
Day and night,
Life and death.
In opposition, harmony—
Without darkness,
Light
Has no meaning.

Yin and Yang
Haikus

. Day breaks, night recedes,
Light dances across the sky—
Darkness softly waits.

> In the stillest stream,
> Both moon and sun find their place,
> Water holds them both.

>> Life and death entwine,
>> Each breath a moment borrowed—
>> Yet given freely.

The Balance of Us
In your eyes, I see the sun rise,
And in your laughter, I hear the moon sigh.
You are the warmth of day,
I, the cool of night—
Together, we are the balance
That makes the stars burn bright.
In every step we take,
We dance between light and shadow,
Never one without the other.
I am your calm,
You are my fire,
And together, we create something
The world has never known.
Like the tides pulled by the moon,
We rise and fall,
Yet we never drown—
Always finding ourselves
In the spaces between.

Nature's Symphony

Branches stretch high,
Touching the sky,
Yet rooted deep
Beneath the soil.
Each leaf a whisper,
Each root a memory,
Both grounded and free,
Reaching for the light
But always anchored
In the dark earth.

The Quiet River

The river flows,
Unchanged,
Yet always moving.
It carries with it
The weight of time,
The echoes of those
Who've come before.
I sit by the banks,
Watching as it twists and turns,
Its surface reflecting the sky,
Its depths holding secrets
I will never know.
Here, I am reminded—
Life is both swift and still,
A constant movement
And yet,
A quiet rest.

The Silent Dance

Beyond the edges of day and night,
A silence holds the world in place.
Life moves in a perfect,
Arch of ebb and flow,
Never one without the other,
Creating harmony in their
Eternal dance.

The Sun and the Moon
You are the sun,
Bright and fierce,
Your light reaching every corner
Of my heart.
I am the moon,
Soft and gentle,
Reflecting the love you give.
We rise and fall together,
Chasing one another across the sky—
Never meeting,
Yet always connected.

The Eternal Cycle
Seasons come and go,
Yet our love remains the same—
Rooted, ever strong.

The Breath of the Earth
The earth breathes in cycles,
As do we.
Our love is like the turning of the seasons,
The steady rhythm of the tides.
There are days when we are as the spring—
New, blooming with color.
And there are days when we are as winter—
Quiet, still, yet holding
The promise of warmth beneath the cold.
In all things,
We are balanced,
Never more, never less,
But always enough.

Tide's Secret

I write you letters in the sand,
Only to watch the tide
Carry them away—
Hoping they'll drift back to shore.
For love, like the ocean, returns
Even when it pulls away,
A promise in every wave.
The tide may take what I give,
But it leaves whispers behind,
Marks upon the shore,
Echoes of everything we've shared.

The Waiting Sky
I gaze up at the stars each night,
Knowing that you, too, may look upon them
And feel the same pull,
The same quiet waiting.
We are bound by the sky,
Waiting on opposite ends,
Yet drawn to the same light.
Though distance divides our gaze,
The heavens keep us connected,
A reminder that in this vast world,
We are never truly apart.

The Garden of Patience

In every word I plant,
There grows a piece of me—
A garden waiting to bloom
In the season of our meeting.
This love, sown in silence,
Awaits the rain of your arrival,
To blossom under your light.
Like seeds beneath the soil,
We wait for time to turn,
To rise together in a garden of patience.

The River's Call
The river whispers your name,
A call that echoes in the spaces between,
Drawing me closer with every turn.
Each ripple a message,
Each current a touch,
The river pulls me,
Carrying me to you.
In its gentle flow, I hear your voice,
A sound as ancient as the stones,
Guiding me to where we meet.

Roots of Us
In you, I find my roots,
Grounding me as I reach for the skies—
We grow together, balanced, whole.
Like a tree and its earth,

Chapter 4: The Language of Love

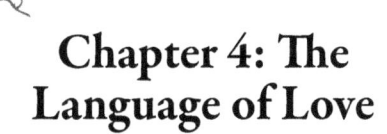

"Love speaks in many forms, not always in words. Sometimes it's found in the spaces between, in the laughter, the glances, the unspoken promises."

Found Poem
Your laugh is the spark
That ignites the sky,
A thousand moments
Woven into one.

Limerick on Love

There once was a heart full of cheer,
That leapt every time you were near.
Though time may decay,
Our love finds its way,
And together, we conquer each fear.

The Color of Us
Red as the sun,
Blue as the sky,
We blend, we blur,
We become something
More.

SOUL

Softly you speak, yet your words resound.
Once lost, in you I have found
Understanding, a love so true—
Lasting, a bond that's me and you.

Message in Silence
In the spaces between each line,
I leave a note for you—
Words not spoken,
But always meant.
Silent syllables of love,
Hidden within the quiet,
Waiting to be heard.
In every pause, I send you my voice,
A language of love that lingers,
Unseen, but always felt.

To the Love I've Yet to Meet

Carefully, I hold these words for you,
Holding them close like a prayer.
Across days and dreams, I send them,
In hopes they will reach you whole.
In silent letters, wrapped in gentle thought,
I lay each word as if building a home,
Where you may one day rest.
My heart beats, each pulse a quiet promise,
Waiting, in love, unseen, yet true.

Secret Lines

These pages hold secrets,
Hidden in the ink's embrace—
They will wait, as I wait,
Until you are ready.
A love whispered in quiet verse,
A language only you can read,
Words woven in hidden codes,
Waiting for you to see,
That every line was meant for us.

Love's Hidden Code
Within every line I write,
A hidden code remains—
A map to the heart you've yet to find.
Each letter is a key to my soul,
Woven in words that hold us close.
In gentle rhythms and silent signs,
Waiting for you to unlock the door,
That leads you here, to where I am.

Ink and Breath

Each word I write is a breath,
Waiting for you to fill its space
And complete the sentence of us.
Without you, these lines are hollow,
Words without a voice—
Ink waiting to breathe.
As I write, I imagine you,
Adding your warmth to each phrase,
Until the page comes alive
With both of us.

Unsaid

What I cannot say aloud,
I tuck between the lines,
A silent language known only to you.
In pauses and spaces, love hides,
Waiting to be uncovered,
Word by unspoken word.
In every unsaid phrase,
In all that lies between the verses,
May you find the truth,
That I have loved you, quietly,
And always.

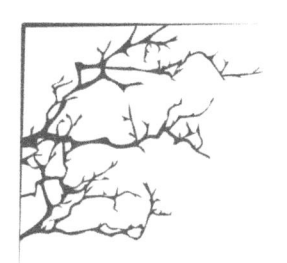

Epilogue

As I close these pages, I am reminded of the quiet, unspoken moments that have come to define my journey—moments between breaths, spaces between words, and the love that fills those gaps. Writing this collection has been more than a creative endeavor; it has been a calling to connect with someone I have yet to meet. These poems are letters sent forward in time, small pieces of myself waiting for a heart that recognizes them.
I hope that as you turn these pages, you find glimpses of your own journey mirrored in these words. I hope these verses bring solace, inspiration, and an understanding of love's timeless nature. Thank you for walking this path with me, for sharing in the anticipation and the longing that pulse within each line.

About the Author

Jaydin C Donough Silent Writer is a poet and dreamer, an explorer of the heart's most hidden realms. Drawn to the timeless themes of love, loss, and connection, Jaydin's poetry is a reflection of a soul seeking resonance in the quiet spaces between moments. Influenced by the beauty of nature and the enduring mysteries of the human spirit, Jaydin weaves words into connections—threads that reach across time and experience.

Please Don't Forget About Me: Tea for My Soul !! is an intimate journey, a heartfelt testament to the anticipation of meeting a love that has yet to arrive, but that already fills each verse with hope and meaning. Through this collection, Jaydin invites readers to find their own reflections in these poems and to cherish the love that exists, both seen and unseen.

Acknowledgments of Inspiration

This collection would not exist without the quiet but powerful forces that inspired its creation. I am grateful to nature, which teaches us about resilience, balance, and the cycles of love that mirror the seasons. The calm of a river, the strength of a tree, the quiet beauty of a moonlit sky—all these inspired the verses you hold in your hands.

I am also deeply indebted to the voices of poets who came before me—Shakespeare, whose words danced through the structure of love, Sylvia Plath and Emily Dickinson, whose courage to write of longing and resilience echo in these pages, and Ella Wheeler Wilcox, whose verses about passion and purpose remind us of the beauty within simplicity. These poets, along with many others, have left a legacy that hums in the background of every word I write.

Lastly, I acknowledge the intangible yet profound feeling of love itself—the unnamed, unseen force that binds us across time and space. This book is a testament to that force, to the hope and belief that love, in all its forms, connects us deeply, even in silence.

Don't miss out!

Visit the website below and you can sign up to receive emails whenever Jaydin C Donough publishes a new book. There's no charge and no obligation.

https://books2read.com/r/B-A-MBFQC-GAUFF

BOOKS 2 READ

Connecting independent readers to independent writers.

Did you love *Please Don't Forget About Me Tea For My Soul*? Then you should read *Tales of Nature Lost among the Thorns*[1] by Silent writer and Jaydin C Donough!

"Tales of Nature Lost Among the Thorns" is a journey through the many faces of love, each poem a petal, thorn, or root that brings depth to the landscape of the human heart. In this collection, author Jaydin C. Donough explores love from its tender beginnings to the complexities that challenge it, and the resilience that allows it to bloom again. Divided into chapters that follow love's stages—from innocence and growth, through

---

1. https://books2read.com/u/bpAvW9

2. https://books2read.com/u/bpAvW9

trials, loss, healing, and transcendence—each poem offers readers a glimpse into love's beauty, power, and mystery.

At just 19, Jaydin C. Donough may be at the beginning of his understanding of love, but the depth of introspection found here speaks to a wisdom beyond years. With vivid nature-inspired imagery and forms ranging from sonnets to free verse, this collection captures love as a force that shapes, challenges, and heals. Some pieces also connect to themes in his previous book, Please Don't Forget About Me, a dedication to a future love, promising that "I've been waiting for you all along." Now, this new collection moves beyond longing, delving into the essence of love itself.

Complete with a glossary and notes to aid readers of all backgrounds, Tales of Nature Lost Among the Thorns is both an invitation to feel love's power and a reminder that every stage—each petal and thorn—teaches us something essential about ourselves. Whether you've loved deeply or are just beginning, this collection offers words to cherish on your own journey.

Also by Jaydin C Donough

Please Don't Forget About Me Tea For My Soul
Tales of Nature Lost among the Thorns